I0465027

101 Sales Insights

Mike Smart

Copyright © 2014 Mike Smart

Gowi Consulting Limited

All rights reserved.
ISBN:150584553X
978-1505845532

Foreword

Firstly thank you to all the people that have helped compile this list of tips, observations and apt quotations.

There was much debate in the editorial team about whether the list should be broken up into sections and related back to various elements of the sales process described in my first book "On A Sales Call". On balance the consensus was that whilst elements of selling are pretty prescriptive i.e. The sales process itself, that in order to become a better sales professional one needs to be able to adapt and change very quickly. Hence the decision was taken to make the list eclectic in nature, so over a case of wine a randomisation strategy was devised and the insights were not sequenced.

So dear reader you can plough through all 101 of the points raised or jump in and scan through and see what catches your eye and imagination. Ultimately, the intention, as with the first book, is to make you think about what it is that you do and how you engage both commercially and in more social environments. There are few right or wrong answers but here you will find a raft of solid ideas and suggestions for you to dissect and contemplate.

Literally hundreds of man years of experience have been brought together to create 101 points; the list could be longer and possibly shorter but the contributors believe there is enough here to keep the reader busy for a while.

Happy hunting and good selling.

Mike

101 Sales Insights

1   If you heat a frog in a saucepan of water it
      will make no effort to escape and allow
      itself to be cooked to death.

   - A great opening gambit to get people
     thinking about complacency in their
     business and personal lives. Not to be
     used with animal activists nor people
     who study frogs – rumour has it they
     will actually try very hard to get out of
     hot water.......still we've seen this used
     as an opening to tremendous effect.

2   A man walks into a square in Montmartre. A
      resident artists asks him he'd like his
      portrait done, the tourist agrees. Ten
      minutes later the man is holding a
      fabulous painting "This is an incredible
      piece of work. How much do you want
      for it?" he asks. "€300 Monsieur" answers
      the artist. The tourist was shocked "How
      much? It only took you a few minutes to
      make." "This is true Monsieur, but it took
      me lifetime to learn how..." came the
      response.

   - Great story for all sorts of reasons but
     the most obvious use is when
     justifying and differentiating on price

and building value into one's own experience.

3   "You can never cross the ocean until you have the courage to lose sight of the shore." – Christopher Columbus

- Very useful to get people to think about stepping outside their comfort zone and providing differentiation for your product or service

4   "Water shapes its course according to the nature of the ground over which it flows; the soldier works out his victory in relation to the foe whom he is facing." – Sun Tzu, The Art of War

- Several very good quotes and tremendously strong concepts in this book. Well worth a read. Water comes up often, its fluidity combined with its inability to be compressed.

5   "To improve is to change; to be perfect is to change often." – Winston Churchill

- One could almost certainly come up with 100 great quotes alone from Winston Churchill's extensive works. That would be cheating, but would recommend you take a look. This quote is all about self-betterment which is terribly important for us all.

6 "More children are born out of wedlock than ever before, perhaps that explains why there are so many bxxxxrds on the road"
- This was a classic quote from a now retired IBM sales manager used to explain why he was late for a meeting.

7 "If you place the order before 30th June I will name my first born after you" – Anon Wang salesman
- In its heyday for a salesman Wang was a great place to work; if you were making the numbers……. This quote does however also neatly demonstrate the "If…..Then" principle of negotiation.

8 "Never give up, never surrender.." – Quote from Galaxy quest, a great spoof of Star Trek
- If you're in sales you need to remember this one…. It's right up there with it's always darkest just before the dawn. You have to keep going, put one foot in front of the other and keep marching.

9 "And the meek shall inherit……."
- No offence intended to those of you of a religious disposition but the truth is that those who do not go out there and make things happen rarely reach

their potential. One needs to get through the noise and being of a "meek" nature is not a wonderful starting point.

10 "Would you tell me, please, which way I ought to go from here?"
"That depends a good deal on where you want to get to."
"I don't much care where –"
"Then it doesn't matter which way you go."
— Lewis Carroll, Alice in Wonderland

- Self-explanatory, if you do not have direction and purpose in life you are going to be on the back foot from the get go.

11 Insanity: doing the same thing over and over again and expecting different results - Albert Einstein

- If it's not working then you're going to have to change your approach.
Simply repeating a mantra over and over again will get you nowhere.

12 "Let silence do the heavy lifting" – Susan Scott, Author "Fierce Conversations"

- Recognise the power of silence, ask a closing question and shut up. Let the prospect explain and don't talk across people.

13 2 Eyes, 2 Ears and 1 mouth

- Best used in that sequence, watch for body language, listen hard to what people are saying and only speak when you have something useful to contribute.

14 Trust your intuition

- Over the years you will have developed, based on your experience, a knack for reading situations. How well you do this will depend on how much you have tried to improve this skill. Your gut reaction is normally not going to be far off the mark and you should behave accordingly.

15 My fair share is 100%

- There is a fine line between winning and losing. Going into a sales situation with less than a 100% commitment to winning is a recipe for disaster. There are few prizes in commercial life for coming second.

16 "The harder I practice the lucking I get" – Arnold Palmer/Gary Player

- Several people have been attributed with this quote or variation thereof. You'll note that they are all top flight winners. Selling is a skill and like all skill it needs to be worked on, refined and honed.

17 Making mistakes is part of the learning process

- I used to work for a brilliant Sales Director, now passed away, he taught me a huge amount. One lesson drilled into me was that making mistakes was unfortunately something that we all prone to do. The point was to learn from them and not to repeat them. Making the same mistake twice is just downright stupid and inexcusable.

18 The world rarely stops spinning or comes to an end

- It's ok to be upset and bitterly disappointed if you lost a deal you believe you should have won. This is a natural and in many ways a good emotion to experience – you'll not want to repeat it in a hurry. The thing to bear in mind is that tomorrow is a new day, with new opportunities and you have to pick yourself up and go again.

19 Be highly selective between using "I think" and "I believe"

- One is a statement of belief. A core emotion, the other is a statement and is typically more easy to change and sometimes if over used can be construed as being aggressive. Language selection is clearly key all the time but consider these two permutations carefully both when you speak and when you are listening.

20 "Show me a vision...."

- In a competitive market one needs to differentiate oneself and one's product. Help you prospective customer join up the dots and see how your product or service can deliver a tangible difference in the bigger picture.

21 Pick battles and win wars

- Not everything you say or do will resonate well with a prospective customer. You most likely will never address every issue to their complete satisfaction, learn to pick those points where you can win and focus on those rather than becoming entrenched and mired in areas where you will never be successful. You want to win the overall debate, not every point.

22 See the wood for the trees

- Too many people fail to sit back and consider major issues and differentiate between what's important and what is general static. This is a true for a customer as it is for a sales professional, so help them focus and agree on core decision points.

23 Focus, focus, focus…………………….

- Every sales campaign has common components but each are unique. Your engagement, your perceived dedication both have to be clearly focused on a single customer at any one point in time. Do not become complacent.

24 Understand that sales is a process

- Read "On A Sales Call", running a cohesive campaign is not fluke.

25 "A long march starts with the very first step" – Chinese proverb

- Firstly recognise the process aspect, secondly that nothing is going to happen unless you initiate the process and lastly make sure that the steps you take along this long path are considered.

26 There's no I in TEAM but there is a lot of ME

- Large sales opportunities by their very nature tend to be complex and involve many people both from the selling organisation and from the potential acquirer. Your team needs a leader, someone who ultimately sets strategy and takes decisions.

27 Quality over quantity

- A prospective customer will not thank you for inundating them with reams of paper that they have to plough through. They're busy people, ensure that you provide concise detailed information and if necessary explain why you have delivered extracts rather than tomes. Tsun Tsu managed to condense a thousand years of Chinese military strategy into 10,000 words, a pamphlet by comparison with some proposals we've seen. Think about it....

28 Inform with a smile and a sense of humour

- It won't hurt and you will break down barriers. Yes, business is a serious matter but it doesn't have to be boring dry affair.

29 Profit, profile, & planet

- What makes someone buy? Consider these points when thinking through the motivation of the person you are dealing with. Simplistically what's in it for the Company? What's in it for the decisions maker? What is the impact on the overall environment?

30 People buy people

- If you haven't figured this out then there is way to go…..you need to work on your interpersonal skills all the time, you need to build relationships across the board.

31 People are all very different

- Please understand this very basic premise, one size does not fit all. You have to adapt your approach to each individual. This is covered in "On A Sales Call" in some detail but there are many studies such as Myer Briggs that are worth taking a read of.

32 There are two sides to every story

- Your position may not be the correct one. The same is true for a prospect, the skill is to understand another person's point of view and then to work through how valid their position is. Clearly they believe or think they are right, they may well be or possibly with a non-aggressive approach you can get them to see another side of the story. Don't ignore their point of view, find merit where appropriate and work through alternatives if practicable.

33 Tell the truth, lying is just too hard…

- One shouldn't lie in business, you WILL eventually come a cropper. There is no point. The best thing about telling the truth, aside of compliance with the clear moral obligation, is that you don't have to remember what you said.

34 Change is the only constant that is a certainty

- One needs to move with the times. One cannot afford to ignore what happens all around us in terms of technology, public opinion, world affairs etc. People's CORE values rarely change but their environments do and one needs to keep abreast of this.

35 Perception is ALL

- Until the great explorers sailed over the horizon the world was flat….FACT. Never underestimate the importance of people's perception over reality. Buying is frequently more an emotional process than a purely scientific factual based exercise. One has to deal with the perceived risk, rewards etc. These need to be influenced and managed as best as possible.

36 Be yourself

- You have intuition, so do your customers. People see through facades very quickly, don't be someone you're not – it will become apparent and lead to distrust. Clearly no basis for a relationship.

37 First rule of holes; if you're in one stop digging.

- Invariably the only person turning a problem into a full blown crisis is the one who created the problem in the first place. Recognise when you are out of position, trying to defend the indefensible or simply made a mistake. The sooner you draw a line and extricate oneself the less the damage will have been done.

38 The difference between winning and losing is a very fine line

- Obvious? Good, then the reader will not need to be reminded that even the smallest details need to be considered, worked on and where possible improved upon. Careless comments, ill-considered asides may all potentially add up and trip you up at the very last moment.

39 Stand by your beliefs

- You are asking a prospective customer to take a risk and give you the business. The least you can do is have the moral fibre to demonstrably stand by what you believe in and not simply be blown around as a piece of flotsam on a zephyr of a breeze.

40 Win win is the best outcome

- A successful negotiation is one where both parties come away believing that they have achieved an equitable outcome. Experience teaches one that it is far better in certain circumstances to give up more than one had to in order to achieve a balanced outcome. The treaty of Versailles is a pretty good illustration of where this basic concept was forgotten, 1939 -1945 ensued.

41 The past is a reference point, not a place to live in – Chris Akabusi

- A great world class athlete and inspirational speaker. His life story is fascinating. We will all experience ups and downs in our life; personal as well as commercial. We should learn from our experiences and move on.

42 Don't be afraid to ask questions, the answers to which you may not like

- In order to succeed in sales, senior management, running a Company or enjoying a good personal life for that matter there is an enormous dependency on you finding out the facts. One simply cannot go through life only wanting to hear good news, if you sense there is a problem then you need to get to the root of the issue/s. How can you make good decisions based on incomplete information?

43 Seek to develop open and honest relationships with those people that you work with both internally and externally

- Want to be the next Machiavelli? Fine, but consider this; most people don't have the talent to carry it off and your customers, colleagues and circle of friends will invariably see through you eventually. It's not a route to long term success on any level.

44 Don't confuse an individual's beliefs with being obstinate

- Sometimes prospects or people generally will "dig in" on a certain point. In order to get someone to change their perspective one needs to establish whether the position held is a rational (in their opinion) or entirely emotive stance. Many individuals like to be awkward for the sheer hell of it, you say "It's black" I say "no it's white". There is no logic, no reason I just want to be argumentative. Alternatively I may have come to the conclusion many years ago that the answer was "white". You need to question very carefully so as to ascertain why I might be taking this position. Try "Help me understand……." Rather than throwing back a hard "Why...?"

45 Questions should be structured so as to lead a conversation

- Careful, considered questioning will invariably help steer a discussion. You will have objectives that you want to achieve from a meeting, think about how to lead into those subject areas through questioning rather than "Can we talk about XYZ now?" Try it, it will raise less curiosity as to why the discussion is moving in a certain direction and will open up a conversation.

46 If it were easy everyone would do it....

- Professional selling is a skill that needs to be learnt and honed. Take pride in your abilities, selling is a facet of every business executive's life whether they carry the word "sales" in their title or not. It is not an optional skill in every professional's armoury.

47 Selling is as much an art as it is a science

- There are thousands of books on sales, some of them are even worth reading. You cannot nor should you ever want to become an automaton. What works for you may not work for the next person. Take the bits of advice in bite sized pieces and digest them, work with them and mould them to your individuality. I don't believe for one moment that reading a 40,000 word book on sales technique would help any more than reviewing 100 or so bullet points.....

48 Patience should not be an excuse to be lazy

- A sales process has a life cycle of its own. It is your responsibility to ensure that throughout the process that your are in close touch with what is going on. There is a balance to be found between being patient and simply sitting by and doing nothing. Your gut instinct/intuition will tell you, with more experience this "feeling" will only improve. As an aside, if you believe that you could do usefully more to move things along then we would suspect that is true more often than not.

49 Picture the outcome

- For those of you that play golf this will be a recommendation that should resonate immediately. Every top golfer would tell you that they try and picture the shot. Try as I might I find it hard to translate this vision of the perfect shot into reality – I don't have the talent. I have, however, found during my thirty years in sales that if I role play in my mind a meeting, presentation or overall sales cycle I can invariably get close to reaching desired outcomes.

50 If you believe that your material, message or delivery lacks punch and is boring – it probably is……

- You should be hyper critical of your performance, work on it.

51 Take a creative stance to problem solving rather than confrontational

- Make clear from the outset that you are looking for solutions that work for both parties. It's a give and take approach that wins in the end. Acknowledge valid concerns and explore the root of the issue, if one looks hard enough with an open mind one does invariably find a way through.

52 Are you clear on the differences between features and benefits?

- You ought to be. Here's a quick cheat add "So what" to a feature, when you run out of answers then you have found the benefit.

53 Clear on when to use open and closed questions?

- Again you ought to be. The key concept is not to create a stilted conversation but to use open and closed questions in such a way as to lead to progress in a sales cycle. Typically you will use open questions to probe, whilst closed questions are there for confirmation.

54 Understand your customers business, their commercial objectives and decision making process

- Obvious one this. Lots of open questions please, do basic research and demonstrate that you understand what your are being told. Learn to use other conversations with similar organisations to perhaps bring in some new ideas and thoughts of your own.

55 Establish a broad relationship within an account

- It's tempting to spend all your time with people that tell you how wonderful you and your product are. Well that's great if they are the decisions maker, budget holder and there is no one else who can get in the way. Most larger organisations tend to make decisions by committee. If you're not covering the bases including those people who are not overtly friendly then you run the risk of getting knocked out and not even knowing why.

56 Social media, a help or a hindrance?

- Well some of what you read on the Internet is true…….. Personally we would recommend caution.

57 Qualify, qualify and then do some more qualification

- Your time is finite. Not only do you need to know that you are seriously in with a chance of winning but through the qualification process you will identify areas of concern. One qualifies on the first call and through every interaction until the contract ink has dried.

58 Pre handle objections

- You know from past experience where problems or concerns are likely to arise. Don't raise issues if they don't exist, but you should know when they are coming. So be a realist and bring solutions to the table in advance. Flush out a likely area of debate early on and determine whether you have a viable solution, it's part of the qualification process but it will also impress your prospects if you demonstrate an open and frank style.

59 Demonstrate that you have an understanding of the risk factors associated with decision making

- Making big decisions in a business is a risky proposition for many people. They need to believe that you understand this and are not simply there to get an order and then walk away. Ensure that your proposal is demonstrably constructed to address risk factors, you are not trying to raise issues but you are a realist.

60 Using trickery is a sure route to failure

- Fool me once shame on me, fool me twice shame on you. The probability of you EVER getting a second chance after leading someone up the proverbial garden path is zip! Not only will you be blighted in that account but your and your company's tarnished reputation will spread. Furthermore people move jobs, particularly as a result of having made a poor decision. Guess who won't be invited to tender next time.....

61 Aim high

- Old adage and has stood the test of time. Applies to how you go after deals, how you work your way through an account in terms of contacts. It will come as no surprise that if you get connections near the top of the tree that people further down the business will be far more willing than is customary to give you time of day.

62 Always leave an escape route

- If you put a person in an unwanted corner with no way out they will fight to the bitter end as they have been left no alternative. You would be well advised to leave a way out, preferably leading to a position that is still in your favour. Done well, they will thank you for it and you still get what you wanted at the outset.

63 Confidence versus arrogance

- A fine line. As a suggestion try to mix in some humility with your very confident approach. People are often labelled incorrectly as arrogant by those people who do not possess such a deep appreciation of a subject matter as the now inappropriately stigmatised individual. Weak people will use the slur as a defensive mechanism. There is not a simple answer, if you preach on a subject that you do not know backwards then you deserve what you get – otherwise stick to your guns would be our advice.

64 Reference sell whenever possible

- If you are fortunate enough to have reference accounts then use them all the time. Sometimes this may not be practical when you are dealing with a direct competitor of your reference account. They may in fact want to do something which is quite different for the sheer hell of it. However, on balance reference selling demonstrates the product works, addresses market needs, other customers have taken the plunge………….Make sure you know about your own customer base, have real life stories that you can tell and drop names that are known in the market.

65 Be prepared to kiss a lot of frogs

- Not every prospect you meet is going to turn into a fabulous Prince or beautiful Princess, dependent on your personal taste. When you are out prospecting you have to go and find lots of people to talk to, you are a hunter looking for an opportunity. The same is true in account management as it is in new business sales; in order to close business you need a pipeline. The first step is filling the prospect hopper with opportunity, be lateral in where you look and go explore. You will know early on, because you WILL qualify, whether the individual discussion has legs or not but at least you will have put yourself in danger of finding a deal.

66 Dry lines catch nae fish – Salmon fishing adage

- In a similar vein to going out and kissing frogs you would be well advised to throw out several lines into the market. To each of these lines, to develop the metaphor, you will want to add some "bait" or a "lure". Come up with ideas about how to apply your products or services to particular needs in the market. Seed these via press articles, public speaking opportunities or targeted email campaigns. You are making unseen contacts, creating waves in a market and hopefully at some juncture you will pique someone's interest enough so that they come of their own volition to you to find out more.

67 Be a realist and engage pragmatically

- No one likes a time waster. If you
  know that what you have to offer is
  not going to be a fit tell the prospect
  up front. If you know that the price is
  going to be way over budget share
  this happy news. Don't promise stuff
  you can't deliver and don't ask a
  prospect to do things which you know
  in your heart he has no chance of ever
  achieving. You are a professional,
  demonstrate this at every
  opportunity.

68 Enjoy your work

- If you don't like meeting people,
  thinking laterally, working hard, enjoy
  the thrill of winning or lack the
  strength of character to pick yourself
  up after losing a hard fought sales
  cycle then you are probably in the
  wrong job. Your prospects do not
  want to hear about your down days,
  they want someone who is upbeat,
  motivated and totally convinced that
  they have the right solution for their
  business. You have a great job and
  this should come across in every
  engagement with your prospective
  customers.

69 Understand your and your competitors strengths and weaknesses

- How can you do your job properly if you don't understand your product in all its guises? How can you focus a prospects attention towards your strengths and away from its weakness's without a detailed appreciation of these plus and minus's? How will you begin to appreciate where you sit in a decision cycle if you have little grasp of how you score against the rest of the market?

70 Never initiate a conversation about your competitors

- Last time I checked they didn't pay your salary, so why are you advertising them? Ask a prospect who's involve in a sales cycle, fair enough. Offer them names, never. If a customer asks your opinion, keep it polite but be clear that your future and career is based on your company's product or service and that's why you are working for them and not another company.

71 Meetings have agenda's and agreed actions

- Be clear from the outset in a structured meeting what it is that you would like to cover, gain agreement that the prospect is happy with this, preferably before you arrive, but it doesn't hurt to confirm in person. Are there any other topics to add to the list? Every agenda ought to have "next steps". Please don't waste your time in front of a prospect, if they come away feeling it was not a good use of their time they are less likely to give you another slot.

72 Beware the "cancerous" issues

- Small problems have a nasty habit of developing into major causes for concern and can destabilise a whole sales cycle. Throughout a sales process be alert to any disruptive theme which continually re-appears despite having been apparently addressed earlier. Invariably the "issue" might be symptom rather than the cause. It could be that the customer hasn't explained the real problem, we haven't listened hard enough. There is something there though and it is really important to get to the bottom of the problem before it explodes and potentially kills the deal.

73 Analyse meetings and outcomes
- Think about what was said, the tone of the discussion and the nature of the questioning. Did you get what you wanted from the meeting? Each engagement during the process has importance.

74 Rehearse objection handling
- If you know your product or service as well as you ought then you should know where a smart customer might start digging. Have your answers ready. When you deliver them please do so in a way that respects the question/objection and add a little theatre i.e. don't answer with a big grin and let on that you were looking forward to the chance of answering that specific point.

75 KISS – Keep It Simple Stupid
- Don't try and baffle people with terminology and complex vector diagrams designed to show how clever you are. Buying cycles and decision making is stressful enough for the people that you are selling to. People want straight answers in

language that they understand. Bear this in mind when you present, it may be all simple stuff to you but for many in the audience you may have lost them at "Good morning….."

76 If you want to get close to a prospect you are going to have to share something of yourself

- It's not a one way street. You want to build a close working relationship? Then you are going to have to be genuine and open up. Ummm, how does that feel?

77 Be versatile in your approach

- One size does not fit all. Your prospects will each have their own preferred method of receiving and digesting information. Take a look at page 36 in "On A Sales Call". Be careful that your style changes, a CEO will interact very differently than say an HR manager. One will potentially want hard facts and be left to draw their own conclusions the other might want to be led through. The title is not the defining issue here, it's the individual facing you across the desk, you need to adjust.

78 Close the deal and leave

- It so basic. You've got the order signed, what more do you want? "Thank you, yes lunch would be lovely but could we please do it next week?" What do you possibly believe you will achieve by remaining there?

79 Engage with your audience

- Do you enjoy sitting listening to a boring presentation where the speaker makes no effort to ensure that he has your attention or is addressing points which are pertinent to you? No? We thought not. Well guess what, neither do your prospects. Think about it and be a harsh judge of yourself.

80 Study body language and be conscious of your own

- Look for basic stuff, arms crossed and snoring during a presentation are normally good indications that it's not going swimmingly. I'm not a qualified psychologist so no expert on the subject but from experience what we are looking for; is the degree of attentiveness i.e. sitting forward or backwards, the folded arms (frequently a defensive posture), hands across the mouth when speaking averted eyes (both could be tells for lying, certainly something not quite straight). Pointing, tone of voice, interactions with other members of the customers "team", who gets heard, who gets shouted down. Be conscious of your tone, what are you doing with your hands? If you're tall try not to tower over someone who is 5ft 2". Try not to look shocked when you get a hard question.....

81 Consciously employ your sales technique

- Over time one does things intuitively which is fine provided that one is still aware that is what one is doing.   The more practised one becomes the more second nature it is to use the skills that have been developed over the years. There is however the danger of becoming complacent and we would therefore urge even the most experienced sales professionals to take the time to think about what it is they doing and why they are doing it. We know from personal experience that we all make stupid mistakes occasionally which occur because we've forgotten basics disciplines. A classic example is giving a prospect answers to problems he hasn't even begun to contemplate. We know they're coming but our timing was, in this case, out i.e. not respecting the life cycle of a sales process.

82 A prospective customer's line of questioning reveals a great deal

- Sometimes it helps to be a "little slow on the uptake" or at least appear to be so. Many times one can hear a question and provide a well-rounded answer. Consider next time probing further around the subject matter before giving the response that you could have initially given. One doesn't have to appear ignorant or daft but a little of probing back and asking for further clarification often reveals a whole subset of questions. It will come as no surprise that in several instance one establishes that the questions were actually planted by those naught chaps down the road, you know our competitors.

83 When possible always use your contracts as the basis of a deal

- It is far harder to insert clauses than to negotiate amendments. Work with your solicitors/lawyers to come up with a set of well-reasoned arguments why your agreements will work well for both parties.

84 What can you use as bargaining counters?

- In complex B2B deals the lead sales resource needs to understand contractual negotiations as well as sales negotiations. This is key to how a commercial deal is structured at the outset and as the process of finalising contracts is worked through. I've worked with brilliant legal resources and with some that were not so great. If you don't want to lose the sale at the eleventh hour make sure you understand your contracts and have a better than average appreciation of how damages work. Understand where there is scope to move, appreciate the revenue recognition issues and where your company is potentially incurring significant liabilities.

85 Appreciate and acknowledge that professional buyers have been taught technique

- You will know immediately when you meet a professional buyer. Typically they become involved late in the process. Just when you think the deal is in the bag along comes Mr/Ms/Mrs Smith and explains how the procurement process really works. Oh joy……. Apart from the obvious observation that you should have known this, for many sales people this is a novel experience. Don't panic, you have your own technique and a professional buyer will see this. Keep calm, don't lose your temper and work through the issues. You're going to have to work with them.

86 Ask for the order

- In "On A Sales Call" page 50 I've highlighted a whole series of closes so will not recap here. Please don't forget as a sales professional you are expected to ask for the order. Your prospect is waiting for you to ask for the order, don't be shy it's your job.

87 Work and social

- In my experience few customers really want to mix their social lives with their commercial world. It's very nice to invite a prospect and partner to the

Grand Prix or tennis but be extremely careful about going further. There is a fine line between building a close working relationship and intruding into someone's home life. Personally I would steer away from it and only become involved at the direct behest of my customer. In 30 years of commercial selling I could count on one hand how many times a social relationship has developed out of the several hundred close personal business relationships that I have enjoyed. I have a lot of friends that are customers but they are "my" friends and not "family" friends. This has worked well for me.

88 You can't win them all

- Losing is a fact of life, it hurts and hurts a lot. In the high value B2B arena where I have spent my career one can't afford to lose many deals because there are so few around to begin with. I would expect to win 2 in 3, a lost deal is not far short of a disaster. We would have invested upwards of $500,000 on some bids so have to be careful where we chose to bid. If you do lose a deal, try to bite back on one's initial reaction of frustration and anger and do so with some degree of good grace. Who knows the winner may fail to deliver……..

89 Into death valley - chasing versus pestering

- The sales cycle has a life of its own. Each is unique, though with common characteristics. There will be times when you will be wondering what to do next. Asking for an update, offering to provide clarification on any outstanding points is all fair game. Be very careful not to overstep the mark. Sometimes you would be far better advised to go off and hunt a new deal whilst the one you are working on is currently in a hiatus. If you are waiting for that promised call to tell you whether you've won or not and really have nothing better to occupy your time go hit some golf balls or go fishing. You will do no good phoning your contacts every 10 minutes.

90 Don't confuse good fortune with silver bullets

- There is no magic to being a top class professional sales executive. Results come from hard work and doing the basics well. There are no silver bullets or short cuts to climbing to the top of the slippery sales tree and believe me it's a long way down. Good fortune happens to those people who put themselves in danger of winning a deal.

91 Never too late to enter the fray

- It's a sad truth that in many cases the organisation that helps initiate a sales process within a prospective customer doesn't actually win the business. This can be for any number of reasons; it's a good idea but their products don't actually fit, they run out things to say during the extended process and the offering appear "stale"; corporate decision making insists that work be done by incumbents. In any event if you do find out about a selection process and you haven't been included then I would always recommend that a) you chastise yourself for not knowing about what's going on in your territory and b) fire off a whole bunch of sales/marketing messages across the account. You will have an uphill battle but at least you know that there is a real project/opportunity on the table.

92 You're only as good as your last sale

- Memories are short in the corporate world. Go out and close the next deal rather than rest on your laurels.

93 If – Rudyard Kipling

- Please read, it will make you a better person and improve your sales technique.

94 Life is a set of joined up inter related experiences

- As one goes through life one experiences a myriad of situations and disparate emotions. One should take the time and makes the conscious effort to recognise that every experience good or bad is an event that one can learn from. The more one learns the better one becomes in a chosen profession and the more rounded you will be as an individual.

95 Acknowledge when you are in the wrong

- Apparently it takes a brave man to admit he's wrong. Ummm, possibly closer to the mark is perhaps that only a fool pretends not to know when they are at fault. Think about it; you deal with highly intelligent work colleagues, friends and business associates please give them the respect they deserve and recognise when you have erred. They most likely know already.

96 Let common sense prevail

- If it sounds daft, could be construed as being legally dubious or seems an overly high risk strategy for minimal return; it probably is.

97 Don't be afraid to ask for help

- Irrespective of how long you have been in business, experienced the ups and down of family and matrimonial bliss you will always find new situations to exercise the old grey cells. There is no harm in asking people for help and in many cases approaching a prospective customer in an open and honest manner and asking for their assistance can deliver unexpected dividends.

98 Be a glass half full person

- Life is what you make of it. Take a positive approach to all aspects of your work and home life. I know sometimes this is hard but the alternative of curling up in a ball and giving up has, at least to me, limited appeal.

99 Be a giver not a taker

- It's a big mistake going through life only trying to figure out "What's in it for me?" You are not the centre of the universe, yes sometimes you have to make hard decisions but these need to be taken in the round and your behaviour should reflect an ethos of fairness towards all people that you deal with.

100 Know when to hold them and when to fold them

- There is invariably always an element of bluff during a sales cycle, particularly when one gets down to the short strokes of the close and contract negotiations. It is imperative to hold your nerve, stand by your beliefs but at the same time maintain a degree of reality. Experience combined with your gut instincts come into play here, there is no mathematical probability to rely on. It's not poker, it's about dealing with human emotions and the practical aspects of what is and isn't going to work for both parties.

101   The biggest differentiator in any campaign is YOU

- You are the person who leads the campaign into new or existing customers. Without you, your company has a bunch of flat products and services. Yes they may be technically wonderful and remarkably well priced but without your drive, commitment and enthusiasm they will not sell. You carry the future of your company on your shoulders, you are responsible for bringing in the orders that pay the bills and keep all the other people employed. You are a professional salesman, the person a prospective customer engages with and who they trust the future of their business with. You remuneration is based on your performance. What an awesome job!

www.ingramcontent.com/pod-product-compliance
Lightning Source LLC
Chambersburg PA
CBHW021050180526
45163CB00005B/2361